Press Releases Made Easy:

Using News Releases to Market Your Business

by Connie Dunn

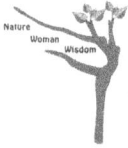

*Press Releases Made Easy: Using News Releases
Market Your Business* © 2012 Connie Dunn
Published by **Nature Woman Wisdom Press**

Copyright © 2012 Connie Dunn
Published by Nature Woman Wisdom Press

ISBN-13: 978-0615723877
ISBN-10: 061572387X
Printed in The United States of America
November 2012

10 9 8 7 6 5 4 3 2

Library of Congress Cataloging in Publication Data

Dunn, Connie
Press Releases Made Easy: Using News Releases to Market Your Business

News Releases
> *Press Releases Made Easy: Using News Releases to Market Your Business
> by Connie Dunn*

Press Releases
> *Press Releases Made Easy; Using News Releases to Market Your Business*
> by Connie Dunn

Writing News Releases
> *Press Releases Made Easy: Using News Releases to Market Your Business
> by Connie Dunn*

Writing Press Releases
> *Press Releases Made Easy: Using News Releases to Market Your Business*
> by Connie Dunn

TABLE OF CONTENTS

Before we jump into the details of what makes a **great press release quote**, let me first give you the bad news. If you are planning on using either of the following phrases in your press release: "We are thrilled," or "we are excited," I have three words for you:

Throw it away.

And don't give me that blank stare because you know who you are.

- excerpt from *How To Write A Killer Press Release Quote*
by John Sternal on March 22, 2010
understandingmarketing.com

WHEN AND WHY
SEND PRESS RELEASES

The main reason for sending a press release or news release is to inform people about something: that something can be a new product, a new program or workshop offering, a move to a new location, and for what other thing that you want the masses to know. Press releases are meant for mass communications.

You can target your market with a news release by sending it to certain publications that would be distributed to your target market. For example, if you wanted to target your market to the alternative health practitioners, you'd send your press releases to publications that target that audience.

Press releases can be a great way to advertise without paying for advertisement. It is not a sure thing that any publication is going to publish your press release. If you need to guarantee that something gets in front of a particular publications' readers, you may need to purchase an ad.

On the other hand, if your press release is enticing to the journalist or editor, they may interview you and maybe other people connected to the story you are telling with your press release. The newsworthiness of a press release is often what makes your story inviting to journalists.

When my youngest daughter was accepted to the Joffrey Ballet's summer intensive program, she needed to raise $5,000. She decided to put on a dance program with some of her friends. First, she needed a place to do her program, which was somewhat easy. Our church gave her the space for free. But you can't raise money without an audience. I helped her write a press release, which the local paper became interested. The newspaper wrote a big article with pictures. But being a freelance journalist, I knew how the media worked. I made sure she sent her press release to all the surrounding publications, as well. And while Internet Marketing has become a huge part marketing today, in 1999, it wasn't huge. Facebook didn't even exist. There was still some ways to use the Internet for marketing. It was more labor intensive. You had to search for places to post information.

If you send out news/press releases every week, you may find that the publications that you want to run them are not as eager to run stories. Fortunately today, there are many other sources to send or post your news releases. Your Facebook page is one place to post such information. While typically your posting cannot accommodate all of what you've written into your news release, you can post your press release on your Website with a link to your full news release. Make sure you put it out on other places, such as LinkedIn and Twitter, as well.

Though you may not gain the eye of the same publication for multiple press releases, you should still send it to that publication. You never know what might grab the attention of a journalist. Also, publications like newspapers have many sections. For example, moving to a new location might be of interest to the Business Section, but a story about you and how you began your business may be of interest to the Leisure Section.

It helps to be familiar with the publications to which you are targeting. While it isn't always practical to have a subscription to multiple newspapers in your area, libraries usually subscribe and make them available for reading. Understanding your target audience and all the publications that appeal to that target is ideal.

Online publications, newsletters, chamber publications, industry publications, and other smaller more targeted publications are all good places to send your news release. Leave no stone unturned! Overlooked opportunities are radio and television. Getting interviewed on either radio or television can give you coverage in audiences you haven't reached with other media. People listen to their radios on their way to work and sometimes all day long. You can send your release to particular radio personalities or just a general release to the station. The same goes for television. If you want to appear on a particular television show, send it to the producer of the show. This information is available on their Websites or the TV station's Website.

For a listing of newspapers anywhere on the planet, go to http://www.onlinenewspapers.com. This website allows you to narrow your search, such as by State. For a listing of magazines by subject, go to http://dir.yahoo.com/News_and_Media/Magazines/.

Newsletters and industry publications are harder to locate online, because there aren't listings of these readily available.

Newsletters are excellent ways to promote your business. One way to do this is to form relationships with people and exchange writing articles for each others businesses. While this activity does not require writing a news release, it is still an opportunity to tell your story, or at least, a part of your story.

Large corporations have marketing departments and public information people to put together marketing campaigns that include press releases. Press packets serve larger businesses by giving publications a more in-depth look at what their business is about. However, smaller businesses can be served by putting together press packets, as well. Solo entrepreneurs have to balance their time and the gain they might receive from creating such a packet. Websites can often serve that purpose.

Press packets include press releases, photos, copies of printed articles, and information about the company. These items can easily be included on your Website. The idea of the press packet is to gather all the positive press. Testimonials are also great to put out on your Website and into your press packet. In fact, testimonials carefully placed in your press release add a lot of pizzazz and personality to your press release. Testimonials in your newsletters and posted on your Website can help those who wish to purchase your products or services to feel comfortable and motivated to complete the sale.

With a little bit of creativity, you will find many opportunities to write and distribute news releases. Press releases can also contain important information that you can add to your Website or your own newsletter or blog.

In today's social media focused marketing, the importance of the news release may not be as obvious as it once was. The good thing is that most publications now accept press releases via e-mail instead of by snail mail, which lowers the cost of sending them out.

According to PRNewsWire.com, you can reach millions by posting your news release online on their site. PRNewswire.com is the industry's most trafficked website, with over 40% more traffic than the closest competitor, helping your message get seen. PR Newswire hosts your release forever, giving it a keyword-rich permanent URL that will help it get found on the Internet's largest search & news engines (Google, Bing, Yahoo!).

- Put your news in front of the 1.5 million unique visitors per month.
- Benefit from PRNewswire.com's highly optimized site structure which helps achieve optimal placement for your release on search engines and, as a result, in front of searchers!
- Capitalize on the 1 million+ referrals from Google each month, almost 400% more than the closest competitor.

Allow your audience to share your message and expand your reach exponentially. According to a study done by Postrank, releases on PRNewswire.com are shared 46% more than our closest competitors. In 30 days news releases on PRNewswire.com were shared 3,218,897 times via Facebook, Twitter and LinkedIn.

- Reach 20,000+ Twitter followers via 20 targeted feeds.
- Take your message viral via our embedded social media toolbar.

For more information, go to PRNewsWire.com

Excerpt from PRNewsWire.com

PRESS RELEASE VS NEWS RELEASE

There have always been some questions about the differences between press releases and news releases, because some people use either word to refer to what they write and send out to the media. Technically, a press release refers to that piece that you send to publications. However, there are far more resources to which you can post your information; therefore, the term News Release is the better word to use in most instances.

Press implies that you are sending it to publications, such as newspapers and magazines. However, in today's technology driven environment, there are so many more resources for which you can post your information. While *Press Release* is still a viable term, *News Release* incorporates much more than just the media. Newspapers and Magazines are just the tip of the iceberg.

In the previous section, I suggested such places as Newsletters, Facebook, Twitter, Websites, and Blog are good places to put the information that you add to a Press/News Release. Being a Guest Blogger or writing a guest column for someone else's newsletter is very much in vogue. The 21st Century has just begun, and more options will come available. Our job as entrepreneurs and solopreneurs is to stay informed and keep looking for other sources for posting our News Release!

Traditional Press Releases - OUT - Online News Releases - IN

Press releases used to be written by public relations professionals exclusively for the media. The media (primarily huge news conglomerates and major trade publications) would then determine what would interest their readers, and/or was 'fit to print'. The editor, publisher or producer had the final say – end of story.

Today companies can gain better control of how their news is distributed, thanks to the online news release, one of the most important marketing tools your company can possess.

With online news releases companies don't have to send news releases only when big news is happening, and only to journalists. They can appeal directly to buyers and most importantly – your news can be used to drive people into the purchasing cycle.

- PRWeb.com

SAMPLE PRESS/NEWS RELEASE

December 23, 2011

CONTACT INFORMATION
Connie Dunn
110 Dean Ave.
Franklin, MA 02038
508-520-3457 * CELL 508-446-1711
connie_dunn@hotmail.com

FOR IMMEDIATE RELEASE

WANT TO WRITE A BOOK?

Are you one of the hundreds of people who want to write a book, but just haven't quite gotten to this project. Well, what are you waiting for? You could have something very important to the world locked away in that brain of yours. If you don't get it written down, it'll be lost.

Nature Woman Wisdom is starting two writing groups in January. A woman's writing group that is being co-sponsored by the Dream Factory, a community of entrepreneurial women who want to realize their professional dreams. This group will be meeting once a month face-to-face for two hours on the second Thursday of each month.

The second group will meet twice a month on the first and third Tuesdays via teleconference and is open to men and women. Because this is a teleconference people can be located virtually anywhere. This is also only an hour at a time, so that people can more easily fit it into their busy schedules.

This group will take writers wherever they are in the writing process and help them get manuscripts ready for publishing. For more information, contact Connie Dunn at connie_dunn@hotmail.com or 508-446-1711.

DISSECTING THE PRESS/NEWS RELEASE

1. The date is the first thing on a Press/News. This is usually the date you are sending it out. This can be the date you are planning to mail it out via e-mail or snail mail.

2. Notice that the CONTACT information is all the way to the right. It doesn't have to be right justified, but these days it is just easier with computers to do it this way. This information is the person to whom questions should be directed. This is important, because often rather than run the press/news release, the publication may want to interview key people. For solopreneurs, this may mean you and some of your clients.

3. This area is for the name, company, address, phone, and e-mail to whom you are targeting with your release. It's important to have all the information on the press/news release so that you can follow up easily.

4. Centered in very bold and capital letters is the date this information should be released. For the most part, small and solo businesses don't plan their releases to be strategically released as part of an overall marketing plan. They should do this, but most small businesses keep most of that in their head instead of writing it down. It would be best to do the entire plan for any product, service, or the overall business, but small businesses are more likely

to market on the fly. If the information is relevant at the time you are sending out the release, just simply put that it is available for Immediate Release. However, if you are sending this out to coincide with a product debut, then you may have a specific date.

5. The next line is the Headline. This line should be enticing yet reflect what your press release is all about. The Headline may be as far as the reader may go as they read your press release, so you need to grab the reader with this headline. A cool tool for helping you fashion this headline is a headline analyzer that is free and is located at http://www.aminstitute.com/headline/. Read the information on this page to fully understand how it analyzes a headline for its emotional appeal.

6. This is the body of your News/Press Release.

USING STORYTELLING TECHNIQUES TO GRAB ATTENTION

Most Press Releases are very dry and to the point, but if you can punch it up, humanize it, and still get out the *Who, What, Where, When and How*, you may have grabbed the attention of the reader. Today more than ever, you need to suck the readers into your News Release! Think of it as writing a mini-article. In a page to two pages, at the most, you need tell the story of what you want the reader to do, feel, smell, hear, experience in just a few paragraphs.

Let's take a look at my first paragraph on the Sample Press/News Release: "Are you one of the hundreds of people who want to write a book, but just haven't quite gotten to this project. Well, what are you waiting for? You could have something very important to the world locked away in that brain of yours. If you don't get it written down, it'll be lost."

In my lead paragraph, I have challenged the reader to do something. I've also drawn them into the storyline of the News Release. Not every Press Release will lend itself to storytelling, but giving it a try may get your information out to a wider audience.

In storytelling, the first thing you need to do is to establish a *hook* or *problem*. My *hook* appealed to the readers' latent desire to write a book. The next step is to *complicate the problem*, which is done by pointing out that they may have some important information that needs to be shared and that if they don't write it down, it will be lost.

The next step in storytelling is to clearly *establish the hero's/shero's goal*. You could say that you do this by giving the reader some options in joining a group of writers to start the journey of writing a book. The last two steps of storytelling are the *climax or high point in the story* and *the resolution*. These two steps are a bit more difficult to highlight in a News Release. However, the point of my News Release was to inform people about my classes. If the News Release were about my business, it would be easier to add these last two steps of storytelling into the Release.

While the storytelling steps may be a bit confusing to you in terms of writing a News Release, however if you focus on just the first step: *the hook or the problem*. Just adding this piece to your News Releases you'll find that they will be less boring and stiff.

Remember that what you need to focus on is how your business benefits your target audience. Therefore, establishing a problem for which you are the solution is always the point of view you need to focus on for your Press Releases. Incorporating any of these five storytelling points within your Release can give your Release the extra pizzazz that can set it apart from other Releases. The five storytelling points are: *the hook or problem; the complication of the problem; the hero's/shero's goal; climax; and resolution.* The importance of attracting notice with your News Release, is why you send them out.

Let's explore how adding the storytelling aspect to your release makes a difference. This is the first paragraph from a sample Press Release for an event:

> *"Morning Mist Health Foods Inc. had its beginnings in Chapel Hill, NC. Now the national chain has returned to the college town to sponsor the First Annual Chapel Hill-Durham Marathon. The race will take place on April, 27th and has already attracted many well-known marathoners, including multi-race winners Herb Putkin and Shelly Walters."*

This is a typical first paragraph for a Press Release. Remember that Press Releases are generally releasing information to the media or newspapers and magazines. News Releases, which are most common today, are not only used to gain attention by journalists at magazines and newspapers but to be run as written in newsletters, blogs, Websites and other alternative spaces to publish.

Let's see how the paragraph can be punched up. More research into the entire Release was actually needed for a rewrite it, because the reason for the race was to promote Morning Mist Health Foods Inc.'s focus on health by sponsoring a marathon. Their Press Release doesn't even state that...so here's my rewrite using the storytelling perspective. Other research was also required to pull together that "hook" or "problem" for the first paragraph.

> Americans are unhealthier than previous generations. With toxins in the air, water, and soil, caused in part by cosmetics, and household cleaning products, we are all at risk for a host of diseases. Foods in our super markets are increasingly more processed and nutritionally deficient.

> To combat these astounding statistics, Morning Mist Health Foods Inc., which promotes nutrient dense foods and supplements is sponsoring the first annual marathon in Chapel, North Carolina, where the health food company began. Joining in the marathon are well-known multi-race marathon winners Herb Putkin and Shelly Walters.

It takes two paragraphs in this rewrite. The first paragraph clearly states the *problem/hook.*, as well as the *complication of the problem.* The second paragraph shows the *hero's/shero's goal.*

With a little creativity and effort, a dull, boring Press Release can be pumped up to tell more of a story. Remembering that Press/News Releases are a marketing tool, we must keep one thing in the forefront of our marketing efforts: our customers and clients aren't interested in what you do as much as they want to know how you are going to solve the problem that they have.

Press/News Releases and Storytelling go well together. The PROBLEM that you SOLVE should easily be determined in everything you write. It makes a better Press/News Release, blog, newsletter article, brochures, flyers, and just about anything you write. You don't always have to beat people over the head with Problems and Solutions, but keeping that in the forefront of your mind as you create marketing materials of all kinds is important. Some would say that marketing is all we really do! Others would say that we tell stories, and that is all we do!

According to E-Releases.com, they contend that PR is Storytelling. They raise the question: How do we make sure we're remembered? Think of your favorite book or your favorite movie. What is the basic outline of the story? What is the plot? The script?

Ask yourself questions as to why this story is so influential. Now ask yourself the exact same questions about your marketing and public relations.

First of all, who is your target audience? How do you want this target audience to feel? Who are the key characters in this story? What is the plot line, or how did you get to the point where you are right now? What is the climax or key success point? And last but not least, what is your conceivable happy ending?

Just like any successful film, an outline is necessary to see the story through to the end. You can't write a script without knowing where you are going to go. Plot out the steps that are necessary to be successful; don't just run headfirst into an unforgiving public.

Make your audience love you, just like the main character of your favorite movie. Make sure you tell a story that will make them connect with you and come back to you again and again.

Excerpt from e-releases.com

STORYTELLING RULES & WRITING BETTER PRESS RELEASES

Everything is a story. When we think about it, we understand that stories are how we communicate, how we make sense of the world around us, and even how we find and define community.

Yes, Virginia, we are now in the 21st Century, but we still tell stories. Some may not look like the classic folk story from our childhood, but we have to understand that even the driest financial statement has at its heart, the story of a company's performance.

When we communicate who we are as a business, we need to engage our audience. We hook them into our story in the same way that storytelling has been done from the beginning our human existence.

In every good book that you read, the first line should be strong enough and enticing enough to get you to read the next line, and the next, and the one after that. When writing a Press or News Release, we have a much shorter time to engage our reader, which is usually a journalist who is story savvy!

There are five basic steps to storytelling:

1. The Hook or the Problem. What is the problem that your business solves? How does that manifest in your audience's life – business or personal?
2. The Complication. This is where you go into detail about their problem and how it effects them.
3. The Hero's Goal. Your Business is the Hero. What is the goal you are trying to achieve in your Press Release?
4. Climax or Highest Point in the Story. At this point in your PR Story, this would be where your goal and your audience's problem connect.
5. Resolution. In a PR Story, this would be where we have brought them through all the reasons for using your services or products and you give the call to action.

Now, you are equipped to tell the story you need to tell in your press release. And beyond the story, of course, you need to give time and dates of events, places where they happen, and how to get more information.

The Who, What, Where, When and How should be answered in your story. If not, you need to revise your Press Release so that it not only draws in your audience but gives the information that is necessary to convey. While your story needs to captivate, it also needs to explain its purpose.

Not long ago, I received this e-mail in my junk mail. I'm not all together sure why I opened it. But I did! It was then that I noticed that the e-mail with a little editing gave me a good example of storytelling for a business purpose .

Here is their Hook: *There is a party, and quite naturally there is a queen of the party. This beautiful woman is always the center of attention and the most popular star of the party.*

The Complication: *When you spend a lot of time getting dressed for a party, you must want to dominate the focus with the best accessories, such as a hobo evening bag.*

The Hero's Goal: *At Alexander Mcqueen Handbags, we have developed a more perfect and captivating look for cocktail parties, formal affair like charity events, and other occasions. These fancier versions are made of delicate leather, patent leather, and a variety of metallics. We've added beautiful enhancements and delicate straps to match your short black cocktail dress or your full length strapless gown.*

The Climax: *As befitting the queen of the party, who brings her leather-based carrier, she does not want it to be connected with other kinds of totes. She finds herself at the center of attention and the most stylish woman at the party. All the men notice and the women avoid her. She knows she has achieved being stylish and the heart of the "in crowd."*

The Resolution: *When you want to be the beautiful woman - the queen - at the core of fashionable trend, you'll buy your bag at Alexander Mcqueen Handbags, which never* sells fakes and invests heavenly in high quality handbags on the cutting edge of style.

STEP-BY-STEP PRESS RELEASE WRITING

Every Press Release needs to answer: Who, What, Where, When, and How. But to do this in a creative method that catches your audience and draws them through the News Release, you need to carefully craft your words. Each paragraph should lead to the next paragraph. If you want people to feel excited about your News, then your News Release should reflect that mood.

Step 1: The date should go on the left-hand side of the page.

Step 2: The Contact information should go on the right-hand side of the page. Give as much Contact information as possible, such as the person to contact, their address, phone (including a Cell phone), fax (if you have one), email and Website address. You want the media to be able to contact you, so help them do their jobs. When you send a Press Release to the media (newspapers and magazines), you want them to contact you and interview you so they will make your News Release a bigger article, maybe even with pictures!

Step 3: The Release Date is centered and should be in all caps. If you are ready to release when you send out your Release, use: FOR IMMEDIATE RELEASE.

Step 4: Before you write your Press Release you want to know: (1) What is the News you want to release? (2) Who are the people (audience) who need this News? (3) Why would your audience want to read the entire Release? How do they connect to your news?

Step 5: Before you write your Headline that goes under your Release Date, write the first 10 words. These are the most effective and powerful words you will write. This is where you can bring in the storytelling. However, do not fall into using big words that most people won't understand. Big words, flowery and fancy language, such as lots of adjectives are not actually powerful and water down the effectiveness of your message. You need to use real facts. If you use puffed up facts to establish the "Problem," media representatives will check facts. Your reputation is on the line with each word you write. Make sure you use facts and attribute those facts to the source from which you found them.

Step 6: Write your Headline. This should be done in larger type than the body of the News Release, centered and not all in caps. However, the most important part of writing a Headline is making it something that draws in the reader of your Press Release. One resource to make sure that your Headline is appealing in the way you want is the Headline Analyzer: http://www.aminstitute.com/headline/.

Step 7: Quotes within your Press Release are good. It can be your own quote or that of someone else, such as a testimonial. Corporations often use quotes from the head of the company. One of the main rules of using a quote is to make sure that it furthers the story you are trying to tell and that the quote is polished, which means that you can doctor or fabricate the quote.

Step 8: Make sure you have given all the details about your news. For example, if it is an event, make sure you have where the event will take place, when it will happen, naturally what the event is. Press Releases used to follow the journalists' inverted pyramid formula, where you put all the "who, what, where, when and how" into the first paragraph.

A press release is one of the best techniques for publicizing an event or calling attention to an issue. A well-written, well-distributed and well-timed press release is not difficult or expensive to produce, yet can be effective and useful. The key to writing an effective press release is getting it read and the information published. With these objectives in mind, the most important elements of the press-release are a clear and engaging text, careful selection of recipients, and good timing of release.

- excerpt from How to Write an Effective Press Release
wagingpeace.org

TIPS FOR WRITING NEWS RELEASES

1. Think about what is happening in your business. Some businesses have more events than others. However, if you are holding a workshop, a course, or another type of event, that is newsworthy. You'll also want to promote the event, so write a News Release.
2. When you hire a new employee, this can be newsworthy. Naturally, in some businesses, this would seem a bit forced. If it doesn't feel right, then don't send it.
3. When you release a new product, this can be newsworthy. This may depend upon the business, but if you are a furniture builder who normally makes certain products and are venturing into another product, it's newsworthy. Send out a News Release.
4. If you are a Service-Oriented business and are beginning to offer a new Service, this is newsworthy. For example, if you are a bookkeeping firm and are adding bill paying services, this is something new. If you are a bookkeeping service and are adding more bookkeeping services than you had previously offered, it still might be newsworthy.
5. If your company has won an award of some sort, this is newsworthy.
6. Another type of News Release would be Human Interest. This would be very specific and directed

more around a person than the business. However, don't overlook this option, because many newspapers have Human Interest sections or pages. They'll fill that with someone, so it might as well be someone in your firm or you. This type requires a bit more work than some of the others. What you have to do in this type of news releases is figure out the Human Interest angle. This entails that you get to know the people who work in your business beyond the 9 to 5 work. For example, if your business was a postal center and one of your employees was getting in shape to run the Boston Marathon that would be newsworthy. The farther from Boston you are the more interesting this story would be, because there would be less people training for it.

7. If your business is offering a scholarship that would be newsworthy at two different times: once to solicit scholarship applicants; secondly when you announce the winner.

8. If your business offers any special programs to students, such as an internship, that is newsworthy.

9. Running any sort of program that will help people in need is newsworthy. For example, if you collect can goods rather than money for say a ticket to your show or a car wash or whatever, this would be newsworthy and commendable!

Just about anything you do that is different will warrant a news release. Do keep in mind, however, that newspapers, in particular, will only run an article about you and your company about once every three years. It may sound harsh, but they want to use the space for others. The Human

Interest story is one of exceptions, because it really isn't about you. It's about someone who works for you. Also the helping people in need story is usually an exception, as well.

Stay plugged in to all the possibilities that you might have to write a press or news release, and do it!

THINGS NOT TO DO

1. DO NOT attach your Press Release to an e-mail. Instead copy and paste it into your e-mail. It will lose some formatting, so try to read through to make sure it is legible and makes sense
2. DO NOT send out your Press Release on Mondays and Fridays or over weekends. The theory at work here is that people cut out early on Fridays. Mondays are a catch up days. Tuesday through Thursday, between the hours of 10 a.m. to 2 p.m.
3. DO NOT use statistics that you have not verified. One great place to check out your Stats is Google Analytics.
4. DO NOT assume that one Release will do the trick. One release will likely not drive tons of traffic and sales to your Website. More frequent Releases, such as one a month, is recommended to

ABOUT THE AUTHOR

Connie Dunn, owner of Publish with Connie, is an author, speaker and educator. Her specialty is self-publishing. She has been writing all her life with about 30 books, screen plays, and curricula. She has taught creative writing, freelance writing, religious education, and a variety of creativity workshops.

Connie's focus today is that of a Book Writing and Publishing Coach, and has taught several groups of people how to write their books and get them published. However, she also offers such workshops as: Book Writing and Publishing; Blog a Book: Book Your Blog; Blogging for Dollars; Behind Medusa's Mask: a Creative Approach to Poetry Writing; and Press Releases Made Easy.

OTHER PUBLISHED BOOKS

The following books are all available on Amazon.com. For more information, go to the Nature Woman Wisdom Press site at http://naturewomanwisdom.com/?page_id=12.

A Spider, Some Thread, and a Labyrinth Walk

Book Writing: Fuzzy About Where to Start?

Goddess Rituals: Reclaiming Our Ancient Spiritual Heritage

Miss Odell: The Privileges of Being Present for the End of Her Life - A Reality Book on Elder Care

The Most Magical, Awesome, Delicate Creature of All

The Real Story of the Dumpty Family

Trees: Peaceful and Personal Meditational Poems